Ways to become a good leader

A Manual for Developing Leadership Skills and Effective Organisations

By Alex Blessing

Table of Contents

Chapter 1
Meaning of leadership

What is Leadership?

In essence, leadership is a constant process of influencing behavior. It could be taken into account in terms of the interactions between a leader and his followers.

To accomplish his aims, the leader strives to affect the actions of people or groups of people around him.

A study should be done on the dynamic process of leadership. It is a relational process that involves interactions between the leaders, the members, and sometimes external constituents. Good leaders may be developed, not born. You can become a successful leader if you have the motivation and willpower.

A crucial and contemporary subject in the area of management practices is leadership development.

In essence, it entails fostering in managers the traits and dispositions that enable them to consider the future and make the required adjustments to various leadership philosophies

1. Introduction to Leadership

2. Principles of Leadership

3. Identifiable traits

14. Future leadership development.

Definitions, concepts, traits, goals, nature, significance, requirements, and leadership skills of leadership

What is Leadership - Leadership is the skill of persuading others to cooperate in achieving collective goals. What a minister does for his State, what a captain does for his team, is what a manager must do for his company. All successful leaders should possess some fundamental traits. They should be able to interact with people on an equal footing, manage and mentor subordinates, settle disputes, find solutions by carefully analyzing all available options, correctly allocate limited resources, and take risks and initiative.

The setting in which a leader is employed is crucial. Different leadership styles may be required in various circumstances depending on the organizational culture, economic and social structure, level of unionization, and other considerations. A task-oriented leader, for example, could perform better in circumstances that are either highly favorable or very unfavorable to him, but a relations-oriented leader would do better in middle-of-the-road circumstances.

"Leadership is the capacity to ignite the desire to pursue a shared aim," says Livingston.

Leadership is the trait of the behavior of persons that allows them to direct others or their actions in organized endeavors, according to C.I. Bernard.

"Leadership is the practice of inspiring and enabling people to work energetically toward attaining goals," said Bernard Keys and Thomas.

In essence, leadership is a constant process of changing behavior. It could be taken into account in terms of the interactions between a leader and his followers. To accomplish his objectives, the leader strives to affect the actions of people or groups of people around him.

Keith Davis once said, "Leadership is the act of inspiring and assisting people to strive arduously toward their goals. To achieve organizational goals, leadership must elicit collaboration and willingness from both people and groups.

Terry, George R. Leadership is a relationship in which one person motivates others to collaborate freely on related activities to realize the goals of the leader.

"Leadership is the process of influencing individuals so that they would strive voluntarily toward the attainment of collective objectives," said Koontz and O'Donnell.

Kenneth I. Bernard, Leadership is defined as "the characteristic of an individual's behavior in which they direct others on their actions in organized labor."

"Leadership is viewed as the shape which authority adopts when it comes into process," said Mooney and Reiley.

According to Alford and Beatty, leadership is the capacity to compel a group of followers to do desired behaviors freely and without the use of force.

The "BE," "KNOW," and "DO" Concept of Leadership: What Is It?

A study should be done on the dynamic process of leadership. It is a relational process that involves interactions between the leaders, the members, and sometimes external constituents. Good leaders may be developed, not born. You can become a successful leader if you have the motivation and willpower.

The continuous process of self-study, education, training, and experience is how good leaders are created. There are several qualities you need to possess to motivate your team members to operate at greater levels of collaboration. These are learned via ongoing labor and study and do not come naturally. Good leaders never stop striving and learning to develop their leadership abilities; they DO NOT take their success for granted.

Leadership is the process through which an individual persuades others to carry out a task and guides the organization in a manner that strengthens its coherence and cohesiveness. Employing their leadership qualities, such as beliefs, values, ethics, character, knowledge, and abilities, leaders carry out this process.

The honesty of character and unselfish dedication to your company is the cornerstone of effective leadership. Your leadership is everything you do that has an impact on the goals of the company and your people, from their perspective. Respected leaders focus on who they are (including their views and character), what they know (including their position, their responsibilities, and human nature), and what they do (such as – implementing, motivating, and providing direction).

What compels someone to obey an authority figure? People want to follow people they admire and who have a strong sense of purpose. They need to act morally if they want respect. By presenting a compelling image of the future, one may establish a feeling of direction.

The "BE, KNOW, DO" Leadership Concept

Act professionally. Examples include demonstrating group loyalty, giving selflessly, and accepting responsibility for one's actions.

Be a person of integrity and professionalism. Honesty, competency, candor, dedication, integrity, bravery, directness, and inventiveness are a few examples.

KNOW the four pillars of leadership: circumstance, follower, leader, and communication.

KNOW who you are. Examples include the good and bad aspects of your knowledge, talents, and character.

KNOW how people think. Examples include basic human wants, feelings, and reactions to stress.

KNOW what you're doing. Examples include being skilled and capable of instructing people in your job.

KNOW your business. Examples include where to get assistance, the area's climate and culture, and the identity of its unofficial leaders.

DO provide instructions. Goal-setting, problem-solving, decision-making, and planning are some examples.

Implement, DO. Examples include talking, planning, managing, and assessing.

DO encourage. Develop the organization's morale and spirit, for instance, train, coach, and provide advice.

Followers, a Personal Quality, a Reciprocal Relationship, a Community of Interests, Guidance, a Shared Function, and a Few Other Qualities are Required for Leadership.

The following are a few leadership qualities:

1. Followers are required:Leadership is nothing without its adherents. A leader cannot wield his or her power if there are no followers. Both official and informal organizations have leadership.

2. Functioning Connection between Leader and Followers: The leader and his followers must have a working relationship. It implies that the leader should show there where the real job is being done. Additionally, the group's dynamic member should be the leader. He cannot do anything if he is not like such.

3. Personal AttributeA man's personality and actions have an impact on other people's creative output.

4. Mutual Understanding:A leader and his followers have a mutually beneficial connection as a result of leadership. Both the leader and the followers have the power to affect one another. The influence is caused by the followers and the leader's willingness, and no coercion is used.

5.Communities of Interest:The leader and his followers need to have the same interests. A leader has personal goals. The adherents have their own goals. In the lack of shared interest, they are headed on distinct paths. It is not suggested. The leader is the one who should make an effort to negotiate between the many goals and balance the needs of the group with those of the individuals.

6. Advice:A leader inspires his subordinates to accomplish the objectives of the group. For this reason, a leader should take action to inspire his supporters.

7. Associated with a Special Situation:Leadership may be used in a certain context at a specific moment. It sometimes fluctuates.

8. Shared Purpose:Leading is a shared responsibility. To help the organization reach its goals, a leader collaborates with his followers. Additionally, the leader

communicates his experience, thoughts, and opinions to his followers.

9. Relationship of Power: A leader has authority over his or her subordinates. The structure of the organization, better knowledge, experience, and other factors provide the leader with these abilities.

What is Leadership? - **11 Key Goals**

Here are the goals of leadership from the perspective of ethics:

(i) To cultivate a sense of coordination and collaboration,

(ii) To identify and provide the necessary guidance regarding appropriate good or poor, right or wrong, conducts and behaviors in society,

To develop new, inventive, and creative ideas, outlooks, and approaches among people. To determine and make perspective visions and missions for the well-being of human life in society. To determine and develop parameters based on ethical values towards optimal and balanced behavior between individuals and groups in any society. To determine some of the following: I To determine the ethical standards that should be followed by individuals and groups in any society.

(viii) To cultivate zeal, fidelity, and devotional attitudes and behaviors,

ix) To identify and provide necessary guidance for fostering a sense of unity among individuals, x) To give proper consideration to a group's or society's shared interests, and xi) To offer some pioneering recommendations for creating a better workplace.

The four defining characteristics of leadership are status group, focal person, function, and process.

Different perspectives on leadership exist (a) Status group b) The main character; c) the function, and d) the process.

(1) Leadership as a Status Group: This term describes a scenario in which a person advances to a leadership position either by election or selection or through heredity (such as when he is a member of a business family).

(2) Leadership as a Focal Person: In this perspective, leadership is vested in individuals who are seen as leaders due to the positions they have within an organization, such as those who are elected or chosen to serve as directors, executives, administrators, managers, or department heads.

(3) Leadership as a Function: \ The leadership function involves acts that support the attainment of group objectives. This task is carried out by someone who is recognized as a leader. The credit or blame for the success or failure of the group effort will be given to the group leader, even though many individuals are working to achieve group objectives, and numerous variables, including luck, impact the outcome of their combined efforts.

(4) Leadership as a Process: In this perspective, leadership is an interactive process in which leaders and followers trade influence. Specifically, the leader influences the followers through his ideas, support, and direction, and the followers influence the leader through their ideas, suggestions, and contributions to the achievement of group goals.

And since there is a favorable balance of influence in the leader's favor, the followers recognize his positional authority, obey his directives in the formal organization, and pay attention to his counsel and recommendations as participants in unofficial groupings. Thus, whether in a formal or informal organization, it is evident that a leader's authority is constrained by the degree to which his followers accept him as their leader.

Defining Leadership and Its Relevance The support that leaders provide includes task support, psychological support, individual development, team building, motivation, and a few more things.

1. Leaders Assemble Organizational Resources and Assist Followers in Task Completion Leaders assist followers by

gathering organizational resources and assisting them in task completion in line with performance standards.

2. Psychological Support: In addition to assisting followers in carrying out organizational responsibilities, leaders also assist them in resolving different issues they face while they carry out these activities. They inspire people to work fervently and enthusiastically. They instill a sense of importance in their followers so that they may complete tasks with assurance.

3. Individual Development: Leaders help followers develop their willingness, passion, and confidence to achieve their own and the organization's objectives. Their general

growth and development as a consequence of this

4. Developing a Sense of Teamwork: No one can succeed on their alone. For followers to cooperate and align their efforts with the objectives and activities of the company, leaders foster a sense of teamwork in them. The team's captain is a leader.

5. Motivation: Leaders encourage workers to take on tasks they would not otherwise be willing to do.

6. Offers feedback: People who are working toward clearly defined aims desire regular feedback on how they are doing, which aids in accomplishing their objectives. They get this criticism from leaders.

7. Aids in the Introduction of Transformation: Strong leaders can persuade their followers of the need and advantages of organizational change. Thus, the process of transformation may be carried out without incident.

8. Uphold Discipline: More than formal rules and regulations, leadership has a strong effect that maintains discipline throughout the company. 9. Affirming Ethical Values: Leadership comes from trust. Members will adhere to laws and regulations if their leaders have faith in them. In a leader, ethics confirms the confidence of the populace (workers, clients, shareholders, suppliers, regulators, and the community). A leader must follow moral principles as a result.

10. Giving Others Confidence: A successful leader inspires confidence in others. It denotes the transfer of power. Today's leader is expected to delegate authority to others rather than keeping full power for himself. He must spread out his influence. To inspire people, he must possess authority and respect.

11. Reviewing the Norms: A leader should periodically review his or her mission and vision statements, as well as any explicit norms and guidelines, taking into account the opinions and experiences of his or her subordinates. This can be done interactively by setting up workshops and discussions, for example.

12. Setting an Ethical Example: Setting an ethical example for others is the greatest leadership duty. Leaders are continually observed and imitated by employees. They erroneously believe that they are free to follow the leader's lead. Regardless of what is written or spoken inside the business, workers often follow a leader's behavior as a performance benchmark.

Imperfect organizational structures, rapid technological, economic, and social changes, the nature of human memberships, as well as a few other factors, are requirements for leadership.

(1) Inadequate Organizational Structure: No organizational structure can create consistently favorable superior-subordinate

interactions. This explains why there are informal groups that function inside official organizations. A formal organizational structure's flaws may be fixed by competent leadership, and formal and informal organizations may be made to cooperate.

(2) Rapid technical, economic, and social change: To keep up with these changes, the company must make the necessary adjustments to its management style, superior-subordinate relationships, and operational procedures.

For instance, it could need to stop producing certain products and services in the case of a decline in demand or start producing alternate goods and services. In the face of escalating competition, it may consider novel strategies to keep its clients and add to its list by establishing a presence in other areas.

It could provide a higher salary package to get more qualified individuals. It may spend more on print and digital media PR and advertising, as well as create promotions like buy one, get one free. It may entice its key distributors with all-expense paid vacations to well-known holiday locales.

It could also invest in new ventures or sell off failing ones. The company can only overcome the obstacles provided by environmental forces with good leadership.

(3) Internal Imbalances Caused by Organizational Growth: As a company

expands and becomes more sophisticated, it may experience certain internal imbalances. Increased organizational activities, for instance, may result in higher layers of management, which may complicate the organization's structure and cause issues with command, coordination, and control of work at various work centers. Only strong leadership can guide a company through such challenges.

(4) Human Memberships and Their Nature:People that work for an organization come from various backgrounds, and they also have various interests, attitudes, and temperaments. Each member belongs to a variety of social groupings that are external to the organization and beyond its control, including families, neighborhood

associations, communities, and social organizations. Conflicts between individual aims and collective interests might sometimes arise as a consequence of such influence.

A competent leader may establish a motivating framework that works to meet the various demands and motivations of each member, so resolving disputes within the group and between individuals.

What Is Leadership? - Person-Oriented, Situational, and Group-Oriented Approaches to the Study of Leadership

There are several methods for studying leadership, but they may all be generically categorized under three categories: (1) trait- or person-oriented methods; (2) situation- or situation-oriented methods; and (3) group-oriented methods. Here, we'll go through each strategy individually, starting with the traits- or person-oriented approach.

(1) Personality traits or a people-oriented leadership style:

According to Traits Theory, a leader should have charismatic traits

The focus is on the traits or attributes of a leader under the Trait or Person-oriented approach. According to Greek and Roman authors like Herodotus and Tacitus, the charisma of certain leaders endowed with special abilities always shapes the path of events.

Conceptually, charisma is more closely related to the way power is used than to actual authority. A charismatic leader is in his position because of personal traits, and he exercises authority without regard to norms that greatly limit it.

leaders are created, not born:

The traits that make a person an effective and successful leader have been the focus of management academics for a while. The result was that the traits hypothesis, often known as the "Great Man" idea, is based on the premise that a leader has unique leadership abilities that are either innate or given to him by God.

People become leaders because, in the words of Linda Smircich and Gareth Morgan, "They can frame and modify events and, in doing so, establish a system of shared meaning that serves as a foundation for organized action." This idea, which contends that developing leadership traits is an impossibility, in some ways challenges the value of leadership development programs.

Personality Traits of a Leader:

The traits method focuses on the personal qualities or attributes of people who may be considered leaders.

These characteristics include some of the following:

1. Size, weight, and skin tone, however, there are a few outliers. A light-weight individual may be a more successful leader than a hefty one, and a person with dark skin can be more effective at leading than someone with a fair complexion. Lai Bahadur Shastri, K. Kamraj, and Jagjivan Ram are three readily available instances of this exception from India.

2. Physical and mental energy; how long he can exert himself.

3. Mental capacity—Having a broad knowledge base.

4. Personality – A charismatic, appealing personality.

5. Initiative—Ingenuity, and bravery to carry out fresh ideas.

6. Imagination: Originality of thought and creativity.

7. Emotional stability—Remaining calm under pressure.

8. A desire to take accountability—the guts to take accountability.

9. Flexibility—The capacity to change with and adapt to new circumstances.

10. Honesty—Openness and truthfulness.

11. Sincerity: Sincerity and genuineness.

12. Willpower and resolve—Determination

13. Persistence – Resilience, and persistence.

14. Endurance—Stamina and staying power.

15. Integrity—Stability, moral rectitude.

16. Determining, final judgment.

17. Courage—Bravery, guts.

18. Physical and sartorial attractiveness.

Analysis of the trait theory:

The trait hypothesis is valid. This is shown by the traits it values in a leader. But it also has many drawbacks.

First, it considers innate leadership traits, however, it does not specify what these qualities are. "Fifty years of research have failed to develop one personality characteristic or collection of attributes that can be utilized to distinguish between leaders and non-leaders," said Eugene Jennings.

Second, it heavily emphasizes the personal traits of leaders while ignoring the traits of followers and the contexts in which leadership is used.

Last but not least, substantial historical evidence refutes it. Although the traits listed in this theory may be desirable in a leader, they cannot be claimed to be necessary. The world has seen a lot of brilliant leaders who rarely had any formal education, as Solomon notes. History is full of untrained, unacademic Fords, Edisons, and Carnegies who didn't even have a high school diploma but rose to leadership positions with a global impact. In terms of the look of good health, do we need to name anybody else than the depraved Gandhi, George Washington, or Carver, the little, helpless black man who was one of America's best scientists? Or, are there many more people who resemble them? Will Hitler or Attila the Hun fail to qualify as a leader if they possess the lofty aims and admirable character that are considered to be among the traits of a leader?

(2) Situational Leadership Approach:

Leadership is dependent on the current environment:

The framework used by the situation-oriented approach is completely at odds with that of the trait- or person-oriented approach. According to it, leadership is greatly influenced by a range of variables, including the leader's personality, his followers, and the current circumstances, which will include the organization's values and traditions, the group's efficacy, the nature of the issue at hand, etc.

The situational approach acknowledges that leadership depends on the interaction of three factors: (a) the amount of direction (task behavior) provided by the leader; (b) the amount of socio-emotional support (relationship behavior) provided by the leader; and (c) the level of readiness or maturity of the followers regarding task performance.

External environmental factors' effects on leadership

The situational method also considers external aspects including followers, work requirements, organizational structure, and prevailing moods. However, it sees followers as the most important aspect because, although they may accept or reject a leader on an individual basis, they collectively decide how much personal authority the leader will exert over them.

Behavior on the Job and Relationship Setting goals, organizing, leading, and regulating are all examples of a leader's task behavior. His interpersonal behavior would demonstrate proper support and encouragement for others, including holding discussions with them about work activities in the spirit of giving and taking, hearing their opinions and complaints, facilitating interactions among employees, and giving appropriate feedback on their performance and accomplishments.

The capacity (job maturity) and willingness (psychological maturity) of followers to concentrate their behavior concerning a specific task will serve as indicators of their degrees of maturity.

Modification of Leadership Style depending on Follower Maturity: The leader's approach must change by the followers' degree of maturity. For instance, when dealing with employees that lack maturity, he will need to adopt a behavior style that is "high on task and low on connection"; he will rigidly "tell" followers what, how, when, and where to complete the duties given to them after clearly outlining their responsibilities.

This is so because the followers themselves lack both the professional and psychological maturity necessary to assume this obligation.

He will need to adopt a behavior style that is "high on task and also high on relationship" for followers with low to moderate levels of maturity. In other words, he will need to sell the message about performance because the followers are willing but unable to complete the task; they have psychological maturity but not job maturity.

He will need to adopt a behavior style that is "low on task but strong on connection" while dealing with followers who have moderate to high degrees of work maturity; In other words, he must persuade followers to "participate" in carrying out the duties since they are capable of doing so but lack the will to do so; they are mature in their work but immature psychologically.

The leader will need to adopt a behavior style that is "low on connection and also low on task relationship" when dealing with followers who have high levels of maturity. In other words, by "delegating," the leader will let followers take care of the duties given to them. The followers in this situation are both professionally and emotionally mature.

Why Managers Like the Situational Approach to Leadership

The notion of situational leadership has been widely accepted around the globe because it provides managers with practical advice on what to do in various circumstances. Its main weakness is its inability to accurately assess the work and psychological maturity levels of each follower, particularly psychological maturity levels.

(3) Group-Oriented Leadership Style:

The group-oriented approach to leadership, which is only an extension of the situational approach, sees leadership as the execution of actions that aid the group in achieving its stated goals. These actions are referred to as group roles or functions. Additionally, it aims to define leadership as "the position one has within a specific organization at any given moment."

Chapter 2

Day to Day leadership role

Different classifications of leadership positions are possible. For instance, K. Benne and P. Sheets have outlined the following 27 distinct leadership roles:

A. Roles in Group Tasks:

(2) Information seeker—Looking for information relevant to an idea (3) Opinion seeker—Consulting experts on the viability of an idea and the veracity of information (4) Information giver—Provider of relevant information (5) Opinion giver—Sharer of own views and outlook with others (6) Elaborator—Expander of ideas or

information (7) Coordinator—Arranger of links between activities (8)

B. Upkeep of Group Buildings Roles:

(15) Compromiser—Agreement striker, balancer (16) Gatekeeper and expediter—Protector and speeder (17) Encourager—Supporter of ideas, activities (18) Harmonizer—Combiner of ideas (19) Compromiser—Agreement striker, balancer (20) (17) Setting the bar high and becoming your own ideal

(18) Follower—Disciple, adherent—Group watcher and commentator—Onlooker and describer (19)

C. Various Roles:

(20) Aggressor: Active advocate, assertor (21) Blocker: Speed controller (22) Credit-seeker—Seeker of recognition (23) Self-assured and accepting of accountability (24) Playboy, joy-maker, and strong influencer (25) Dominator, supporter of unusual ideas (26) Help seeker, assistance pleader

As a result, a leader takes on several roles, each of which has a specific goal in mind. Furthermore, different people may take on the role of leader at various times to guide the actions of their group members.

Leadership Definition and Leadership Effectiveness

In a corporate setting, managers at different levels take on leadership positions in their relationships with their subordinates to get the right things done in the right way to accomplish a certain set of objectives. The existence and prosperity of an organization depend on how well managers lead. Therefore, leadership effectiveness is highly valued in the corporate world.

On the factors that determine a leader's efficacy, there are at least three primary points of view. One perspective is that an individual's capacity for leadership depends on their attributes or qualities. Although having these traits does not ensure effectiveness, we can only state that they raise the likelihood of successful leadership.

According to the second point of view, a leader's efficacy is determined more by what they do and how they act than by who they are. The behavioral approach is what is used in this. Productivity orientation and employee happiness orientation are the two key facets of a leader's behavior. Effective leaders are those that have extremely high scores in both of the aforementioned behavioral aspects.

They place the organization's responsibilities and objectives on par with its workers' significance. High productivity and employee happiness are valued by effective leaders as being consistent with and beneficial to one another.

The third perspective holds that at least three factors—the leader, the followers, and the job circumstances—interact to determine how successful a leader is. The situational or contingency approach to leadership is what is meant by this. Specifically, job completion and follower satisfaction are used to determine efficacy.

It is based on the characteristics of the leader, his position of authority or power (how much power or authority he holds, the extent of his knowledge, skill, and competence, and the degree to which he can use them), the goals, attitudes, and abilities of the group members, and the task circumstances. It is also influenced by technology, organizational or task structure, the relationship between tasks, the division of labor, the freedom available for carrying out the tasks, the level of imposed control, and the degree of resistance.

The capacity of the leader to adapt diverse behavioral types to fit different circumstances is crucial to successful leadership in this scenario. There is no one optimal leadership style that works in every circumstance.

We may draw the following conclusions after carefully analyzing the three opinions on the factors that influence leadership effectiveness that was previously discussed:

(A) To be an effective leader, a person must possess a few fundamental traits. Although essential, they are insufficient.

(b) There isn't a perfect way to lead or act that works in every circumstance. By adapting one's style to the needs of each circumstance, one may maintain or improve one's leadership effectiveness.

(c) Task complexity, the knowledge and attitudes of the group of followers, their relationships with the leader, and the position power of the leader himself are significant situational aspects that have an impact on leadership effectiveness.

Leadership: Definition and Leadership in Two Cultures: Egalitarian and Hierarchical Cultures

In a competitive environment, a contemporary organization's staff is a synthesis of several cultures. Employees from various ethnicities, speaking various languages, and adhering to entirely distinct cultural standards, may work for the same company. As a result, a variety of cross-cultural problems have arisen that may have an impact on the workplace culture of a business.

Due to cultural differences, employees of a company find it challenging to work in other nations. A leader in this situation has to be skilled at resolving cross-cultural problems.

According to a leader's viewpoint, organizational cultures may be classified as egalitarian/equalitarian or hierarchical.

Let's go through each of them in further detail:

1. Egalitarian/Equalitarian Culture: An egalitarian/equalitarian culture accords equal status to all people, regardless of their racial or ethnic background, age, or gender.

Leaders in these societies display the traits listed below:

They must attend to their subordinates' flexible work needs since they

 i. prefer self-direction and

ii. want no or little supervision from anybody.

iii. Need to have reasonable expectations, understandable rules, and a general conscience.

i v. Need to treat all subordinates with respect and mutual trust.

v. Need to be honest and cautious when dealing with subordinates because they believe in reserving their rights so that they can challenge authority when necessary.

2.   Hierarchical   Culture: A hierarchy-based culture upholds social hierarchy. For instance, high-status individuals set themselves apart from low-status individuals. Some individuals have positions of authority, while others must comply with their requests.

In a hierarchical society, a leader:

i. Gives his or her subordinates precise instructions

ii. communicates the duties and responsibilities of subordinate.

iii. Usually uses authority to persuade subordinates

iv. Enforces the policies, procedures, and regulations of others subordinates

How to Develop Leadership Skills: Have a Vision, Make Decisions, Take Risks,

Motivate Others, Build Teams, Process Self-Knowledge, and a Few Other Things
Leaders don't emerge out of anywhere. Even "born" leaders don't naturally have all these abilities.

Being a strong leader requires that you:

1. Have a Vision: Leaders are clear about their goals and how they plan to achieve them. They take in the entire picture before developing a strategic strategy to reach their objectives. Find out how to expand your view - Make friends with influential businesspeople in your town (not only those in real estate), study biographies of great executives and current and classic business literature, and create a mission statement for your firm.

2. Decide: Because they have faith in their talents and themselves, leaders don't hesitate to take on challenging or controversial choices. They are aware that

procrastination squanders chances and resources. Developing your decision-making abilities by practicing in situations when failing isn't crucial to building your confidence. If a choice proves to be incorrect, take the lesson to heart and proceed.

3. Take Chances: Leaders have the guts to take action when the outcome is uncertain. They will take the chance of failing. Become more risk-averse - Analyze the issue, describe the benefits and drawbacks of each option, and then rate the level of risk associated with each option from 1 to 5. Next, calculate the odds that each result will materialize. You may use this to decide how much risk you want to accept. TIP - Don't strive for excellence. Nobody consistently succeeds. Leaders learn from their errors.

4. Motivate Others: Leaders can persuade others of the merit of their ideas by clearly articulating their vision and values. They

have the power to motivate individuals to work together toward shared objectives and accomplish feats they never dreamed possible. Discover the many requirements that drive individuals and acknowledge that not everyone is motivated by the same incentives as you. To find out what drives people, pay close attention to what they say. Make sure your staff members comprehend how their efforts contribute to a greater cause to inspire them.

5. Develop Teams: Effective leaders develop teams that bring forth the best in individuals. They successfully teach teams in cooperate, reach agreements, and handle conflicts. Find out how to develop your team-building abilities - Never respond to a question with a predetermined notion. Instead of only attempting to make your point during debates, focus on recognizing other people's points of view. The secret to developing a great team is the same desire to involve others.

6. Self-awareness: Leaders can analyze their actions objectively and are aware of their advantages and disadvantages. They own their flaws, are receptive to criticism, and are prepared to change when called upon. Learn how to increase your awareness of yourself. Learn about your behavior and the impact you have on others by paying careful attention to yourself and using self-evaluation strategies. Seek feedback from others on your leadership style, including any critiques or suggestions for improvement. TIP - Keep a notebook of significant events; review it afterward to see what went well and what you may have improved.

7. Show Integrity: Leaders must be dependable in the eyes of those who follow them. Competence, consistency, care, honesty, and congruity—which he describes as genuineness, dependability, and feeling comfortable with oneself—are traits that

build trust. Find out how to evaluate your honesty. To find out whether your beliefs and feeling of responsibility align with those of your peer group, actively seek input from friends, coworkers, and even employees.

8. Pursue Lifelong Learning: Leaders are willing to learn new things and are receptive to them. Find out how to increase your knowledge - Keep a wide perspective. For ideas and inspiration, go outside of your company and sector, and study books on cutting-edge management concepts. TIP - Astute managers seek partners or assistants who can strengthen their areas of weakness.

9. Effective Communication: Leaders may express their views to a variety of people and change their communication methods to suit the demands of the followers they are responsible. Learn to communicate more effectively - Practice active listening and other communication skills. When speaking with subordinates who may be hesitant to

express their opinions, be sure to read between the lines. To be confident that you have conveyed your idea clearly, restate crucial points numerous times or request that the audience repeat them back to you.

10. Encourage Others to Succeed: Leaders encourage others and go above and beyond to help them realize their full potential, which is advantageous to the business. Encourage others by mentoring those who you believe have the potential to take on leadership responsibilities.

What Is Leadership? Differentiating Between Headship, Domination, and Leadership

Leading is an Informal Process:
Headship or dominance is not the same as leadership. Placement in positions of official power or responsibility within an organizational structure is referred to as headship. Due to his election or

appointment to the office, the head may have a position of official power or authority. This might be because his electors or selectors want him to hold that position, or it could be because his family owns the organization and he just so happens to be the head of that family by accident of birth.

A family head's exercise of power, for instance, does not automatically make him the leader of the family's members or the subordinates in an educational or military institution. Only because he is the leader of the family, school, or military group is his authority recognized. Only if they accept him as the leader will he have a big impact on how these organizations' members behave.

(2) Leadership is fundamentally an influence process, not always a manager directing subordinates to achieve stated goals A manager is functioning as the head, yes, but not necessarily as a leader, when he

instructs his staff to work toward predefined goals. Only because he has managerial control over them and not because they respect him as a leader would subordinate follow his directives.

Because they perceive him as a useful tool for achieving their own and the group's needs and desires, subordinates readily accept the authority of the leader, whose influence is extremely strong. A group only accepts leadership on its terms, to put it another way.

(3) Dominant Leadership Suppresses Innovation: If a leader abuses the authority granted to him by his position, he will stifle the creativity of others who are a part of his organization. When he talks, his team won't participate; they won't share their opinions on how a new strategy or approach to the job will produce greater outcomes. A real leader is like a conductor of an orchestra waving his baton to guide musicians on

various instruments while facing away from the audience.

What Is Leadership and Recent Advances in Leadership: empowerment, direction Planning for succession, coaching, and the role of technology
In today's competitive environment, the idea of leadership has undergone a significant transformation.

The following points describe how multifaceted duties are demanded of modern leaders in organizations:

1. Empowerment: This entails giving workers control over their work. It is encouraged to share authority and responsibility with subordinates for a leader to be successful. In an environment of empowerment, managers must solicit proposals from staff and delegate authority. In smaller, less bureaucratic businesses, empowerment is the most straightforward

to execute. Employees are given the chance to take initiative via empowerment.

2. Leadership Succession Planning: Deals with identifying potential leaders and making sure they keep improving. Finding talent inside a company and encouraging it to thrive in whatever they do as well as inspiring others by setting an example are both facilitated by succession planning.

3. Coaching: Suggests that leaders should provide staff instructions, direction, advice, and encouragement to help them execute their jobs more effectively. This is the job that a leader now plays, but it is still not widely, consistently, and visibly used. According to several writers, coaching is a technique for leading, teaching, and training a person or a group to achieve certain objectives or develop certain abilities.

4. Technology's Importance: This shows how dependent on technology today's enterprises are. With the development of

technology, decision-making has become increasingly result-oriented and time-bound. A contemporary leader is required to be completely aware of the effects of technology both within and outside the firm.

Future Leadership Development:

A crucial and contemporary subject in the area of management practices is leadership development. In essence, it entails fostering in managers the traits and dispositions that enable them to consider the future and make the required adjustments to various leadership philosophies.

A recent focus in the management profession has been on the development of leadership via many cognitive and behavioral facets. It mostly depends on how CEOs and other leaders are growing personally within the framework of collective dynamics.

Here are the components for several elements of leadership development:

In the current corporate environment, it is important to study and comprehend the traits and capacities of leaders.

 (i)It is also important to be aware of one's strengths and limitations as well as any potential development areas for complementary talents and strengths.

(ii) Through self-improvement, it is possible to develop the fundamental qualities of a leader;

 (iii) it is also possible to create a learning process for learning about the various sociocultural environments and the wide variety of lifestyles in society; and

(iv) it is possible to learn these things.

In the process of developing leaders, it is important to avoid and discourage autocratic behavior, monopolistic attitudes, social evils, resistance to change, unethical organizational norms, and various critical organizational approaches.

(V) Emotional competencies also foster and sustain trust, empathy, belongingness, and morale value.

(vi) The financial support for continuing education and training programs must be provided,
(vii) The leadership styles may develop a humanitarian foundation that is properly based on employee-oriented aspects in the organization,
 (viii) To provide rewards and appreciation for those who develop new concepts, improvements, and are innovative, and

(ix) To develop proactive in creating a learning organization that embraces new visions, approaches, and openness.

Chapter 3
Growth in leadership
Five Characteristics Of Growth Leaders

Growth leaders stand out for both their deeds and personal qualities. These particular qualities, which are more akin to personality characteristics than actual managerial abilities, eventually foster trust.

Timely

I deal with individuals who claim they wish to expand their business, neighborhood, or group every day. And I am certain that they mean it. But how people choose to spend their time and that of others often stands in the way of their advancement. When I examine how individuals spend their time, I see that they often fall back on what they are most familiar with. They spend their days concentrating on the projects they are most adept at finishing.

Successful leaders, on the other hand, focus their attention primarily on the areas that need it. They decide as soon as a choice is required, neither more nor less often.

Time shouldn't be spent with activities only for the sake of doing them. Leaders are adept at setting priorities to have an effect because they are aware of the nature of time. They are aware that being punctual is not the result of Day-Timers, working longer hours, or taking on more work. Some people naturally possess this skill. Others see it as a leadership trait that has to be developed through practice. But make no mistake, understanding the value of time is a must for leading a development surge.

Most managers just get up and go about their business. Growth leaders get up and take action when necessary.

Realistic

Many people make fun of reality. Putting on our rose-colored glasses and just seeing what we want to see is undoubtedly simpler. Growth leaders may be identified by their relentless attention to what is and what is capable of becoming. While positive thought has its purpose, illusions are harmful.

"The best product is ours," "Our squad is the best," "Our clients adore us." The importance of our cause exceeds that of all others. Really? Let's trash the T-shirts, tear down the banners, and can the meaningless catchphrases. It takes a realist today to distinguish the truth from conventional groupthink.

Being realistic is not only a nice idea; it is a leadership need. Your organization is dependent on someone to question the current most deeply held ideas of the organization. Why couldn't a leader like you do that? We keep deeply held ideas on our bookshelves far too long after they have outlived their usefulness. Growth leaders accept any reality checks and just seek the truth.

Unscripted

Today, there are many doubters around the globe. Simply said, people are cynical, and why shouldn't they be? We have seen discredited international leaders, questionable armed wars, stolen pensions, and "new and better" items that are neither new nor improved during the previous 50 years. We live in a society where organizations often provide us with spin, misinformation, and falsified half-truths. Any leader in the twenty-first century should realize that many people are hesitant to trust anything. Everyone has a very accurate garbage detector.

Our desire is sincerity. We need leaders who communicate, authentically, and without using talking points. We want managers who disapprove of corporate speak.

Professionals that don't cover themselves with buzzwords are what we're looking for.

Mastering sincerity is essential for leadership. Avoid using the newest buzzwords and outdated clichés; instead, speak what you mean and mean what you say.

Sensitive

It's a strong phrase. Although the word has several meanings, I'm using "perceptive" here. Sensitive leaders are excellent observers and are fully aware of their environment. They have a natural talent for perceiving people's intentions. Long before the real storm, they can sense the barely audible gusts of change. They have an amazing talent for making sense of apparently unrelated facts.

How adeptly do you interpret people in challenging social settings? How much do you believe your instincts? How effectively are you able to manage your own and other people's emotional outbursts? What is your ease of transition from perception to action?

These kinds of talents come naturally to the majority of development leaders. Others must routinely take time away from their daily tasks to practice these leadership qualities. In any case, having sensitivity provides leaders with another tool in their quiver for organizational development.

Transparent

Human nature dictates that we don't trust individuals who try to keep information from us. For instance, when an organization has a PR crisis and begins to decline, it almost always has something to do with not being honest. The majority of the significant business and governmental scandals of the modern era have been more about cover-ups than actual wrongdoing.

On the other hand, those individuals and organizations who are open about their activities tend to flourish over time and outperform the competition. People who are open with information, both positive and negative, are better able to lead a group of people to achieve great things.

An organization may and should be transparent on its own, but to do so, it needs transparent leaders. A lively hive of bees I find it quite menacing looking hanging in a tree. I don't believe it in any way. But have you ever seen a beehive in cross-section? We may see the intriguing internal operations of a successful organization by enclosing it in a glass.

Transparent leaders set expectations that are known by their team members, clients, suppliers, and shareholders. It needs confidence and dedication to promote openness. Although it might be tempting to cover up issues, the honest leader understands that the truth ultimately comes to light and often seems worse than it did at first. Three things, the sun, the moon, and the truth, cannot be kept concealed forever, according to an adage from the East.

Chapter 4
Clarity and Transparency

Today's corporate leaders must guide their workers through a novel and often unexpected work environment; this mission will need openness and clarity at every point.

Employees have learned what it takes to be productive over a protracted crisis, regardless of whether they have been working from home or have never left the front lines. Employees have had to adapt to considerable changes in where, how, and how they work, in addition to having valid worries about their health and safety, as well as the safety of their families and friends.

Business leaders of today must now assist their employees in navigating a new, often uncertain work environment. Transparency and clarity in communication are essential components of our objective.

Workers anticipate being informed

Employees anticipate that their managers will notify them about developments inside their firms. This entails having open discussions with workers about how the business is being affected, the company's reaction, if employment may be affected, and what they can do to help the organization survive, if not thrive, during these trying times.

Workers want to know what is going on from their managers so they are not caught off guard. Leaders should always be upfront and sincere about their motives and behavior. Leaders must also be aware that excessive sharing might unintentionally result in tension and worry. Leaders should aim for what I refer to as "responsible transparency" to create a healthy balance.

responsible disclosure

Although giving workers access to the many and sometimes overwhelming factors that go into making a choice frequently results in additional uncertainty and turmoil, it's usual for employees to demand more insights and a sense of direction from their leaders. Important information might also be misunderstood if it isn't conveyed genuinely and straightforwardly. Employees could also perceive it incorrectly if this happens. In contrast, a strategy that prioritizes responsible transparency empowers leaders to stop and provide accurate, relevant information that is simple to grasp and consume.

Let's take the hypothetical situation where you are deciding whether workers will report back to the workplace. Safety should always come first, but you should also think about company culture and how this choice can affect sustaining or strengthening it. It may be necessary to share a lot of data with workers for the sake of openness, but is it the best course of action?

Instead, they might simply announce the outcome and list some of the most important and deciding elements that went into the decision-making process. Our ultimate objective with responsible transparency is to provide workers with the appropriate information at the appropriate time so they may independently come to wise, data-informed choices.

For leaders who believe they should always be able to provide their employees with an explanation for their actions or who don't feel comfortable doing so, this strategy may be a shift. Instead, we are empowering our leaders to express the choice with clarity, which lowers tension and worry for everyone, by providing the precise benefits and drawbacks of the options that went into the final decision.

Leaders need to be real as well as open. They must shun "corporate-speak" and talk in their voices. People dislike being talked "at," and they can spot it when it occurs. For instance, our workers have been through a prolonged period of stress and upheaval at both work and home. People want to know that we see them as fellow humans, that we understand that we all participate in the human experience, and that, to be honest, it hasn't always been a pleasant one.

Also important to employees is leadership listening. Communication must take place in both ways for empathy listening to take place. As leaders, we must be receptive to our team members' questions and concerns, show empathy in our responses and utilize these conversational insights to increase understanding to ensure that everyone feels heard. In other words, "Empathy + Compassion = Mutual Understanding" is the success formula for successful listening.

providing communication clarity
Adopting responsible transparency may greatly assist leaders in being clear when speaking with employees about changes. Employees are better able to comprehend the circumstance or work at hand when given data and facts. Their confidence in the company and willingness to support the desired course of action tend to grow.

Employees will get used to this style of communication if leaders start using it. It requires an intentional mentality to communicate messages, choices, and updates in a manner that captures people's hearts and minds while upholding responsible openness. If there is anything we have learned over the last 18 months, it is that if we don't give people a sense of being seen, heard, and appreciated, we risk losing them.

For better transparency and clarity, leaders should emphasize being direct, honest, and sincere in their conversations with staff members and making it clear what is changing and what is staying the same. By doing this, we can establish personal connections with our employees and win their support for upcoming changes.

The last two years have been tough, but they have also taught us what it takes to help our colleagues through adversity: honesty, empathy, compassion, and understanding. This trust becomes a key component of motivating your workforce to collaborate with you in pursuit of your joint objectives when they are aware that they can rely on responsible openness and clarity in your communications. As we advance in this dynamic and always-changing workplace, you can remain the same and support the success of your team members and your company.

Chapter 5
Ways to become a good leader

8 Ways to Improve Your Leadership

Most of us have worked under a challenging supervisor who constantly focused on our flaws and made us hate coming to work. More significantly, some of us could have had the good fortune to work under a strong supervisor who respected us, listened to us, and inspired us. In general, the former causes poor morale and a high rate of staff turnover. The latter will foster a high-performance culture and boost staff productivity. What makes a difference, then? Why does one lead effectively while the other does not?

How to Lead others

The great majority of effective leaders are taught, however, one in a million people may be born leaders. A graduate degree is often required for those who want to work in management. You will learn the information and abilities necessary to become a leader at Ottawa University. The eight traits of effective leadership listed below will motivate you to succeed as a leader.

1. Act as a compassionate leader

The most important quality in a leader is empathy. Unfortunately, a lot of executives lack formal leadership training and were elevated to their roles based on prior performance or professional qualifications. The end consequence may be a bossy, directive manager who lacks empathy for their staff and sets confusing expectations. Low morale and productivity are often the results.

Being sincere with your team shouldn't entail being close with everyone on it. It entails sharing our shared human experiences, tearing down barriers of defense, and demonstrating your humanity. It helps you get respect and makes you look more accessible. Are you still in charge? Yes, however, staff members are far more inclined to provide and accept candid criticism if there is reciprocal respect and empathy shown.

2. Listen intently.

Everyone wants to be heard, right? Along with empathy, a good leader respects the opinions of the people on his or her team, is curious about what makes individuals tick, and assists them in setting and achieving professional objectives. Will you consistently concur? Of course not, but you will gain a lot of respect and loyalty if you show them that you appreciate them by paying attention to what they have to say and responding accordingly. Exists a dispute with another employee? Deal with it as soon as you can. Is there a crisis in the family? Give them a method to change their work schedule without fearing for their employment.

Don't overlook how beneficial it might be to listen to employee input. Let them know when they have excellent ideas! The more you can establish a professional rapport with your workers, the simpler it will be for them to be open and honest about the constructive changes that need to be done.

How to Lead Effectively at Work

3. Act as an example of accepting change.

The finest leaders may be derailed by change. A recent survey of 1,000 senior executives revealed that managing change and innovation was the biggest issue for CEOs. Therefore, developing the ability to lead through change is a crucial talent for leaders, whether they are implementing new rules and procedures, introducing a new business model, or adjusting to the leadership style of a new CEO. Effective leaders set the bar for how to proceed by modeling a positive and professional reaction to change. Future leaders are prepared in this crucial area of leadership via Ottawa University's Master of Arts in Leadership and MBA programs.

4. Include a common vision

Because the commander has made it abundantly obvious what they are fighting for and what the stakes are, a top general should not fear that the warriors will follow them into battle when the cry is uttered. A visionary corporate executive will follow suit. Each employee has to be aware of the significance of their work. Employees who have a say in organizational decisions are more likely to comprehend the motivation behind the organization's vision and to support its objectives. In other words, workers back what they contribute. Understanding leadership principles will thus help people come together around a common goal.

5. Increase your fan base

It's critical to support your team. High-performing teams are created by leaders who are aware of how different positions interact with one another and who maintain open lines of communication. Tell them you value what they have to offer. A dedicated leader equips their team with the knowledge, abilities, and resources necessary for them to perform their duties successfully. The best way to do this is by offering professional development. Additionally, if you think they have the potential, give them chances to use their abilities in novel ways or encourage them to take the reins and run a meeting or project. They'll realize that obtaining credit isn't the only goal.

6. Express clear expectations that are practical.

When they are penalized for failing to perform something that was never clearly explained, too many workers get irate. Effective leaders establish specific objectives to be fulfilled, clear expectations of what happens if they are or are not realized, and a roadmap for completing the task at hand rather than just expecting workers to perform their duties. Achievable objectives are determined by evaluating all the variables that go into their achievement by effective leaders. Employee morale falls when the failure occurs often. On the other hand, praising them when objectives are accomplished and offering constructive criticism encourages them to keep up their hard effort.

How to Be an Outstanding Leader

7. Develop your capacity for failure

Life includes failure. The way you manage it as a leader sends a powerful message to your team. It is often ineffective to act in anger and point fingers. Instead, discuss with your team what went wrong and what might have been done differently to assure success if you want to learn how to be a great leader. Accept responsibility for whatever role you may have had in the goal being missed. Identify areas that may be improved moving forward as a group. And with mercy, hold workers responsible when necessary.

8. Keep going to school

Since there is no such thing as a perfect leader and change are a constant, it is crucial for leaders to continuously develop their abilities and keep up with business trends. You should assess your leadership skills, as well as their strengths and flaws if you want to learn how to become a leader or develop your leadership style. To assist you in doing this, there are several evaluation tools available. Once you've determined the areas you want to improve, it's time to pick up some new habits.

Gaining an online, expedited degree from Ottawa University is a great approach to developing your leadership abilities. With a Bachelor of Arts in Human Resources, you could want to nurture and demonstrate leadership on the administrative side. With a Master of Business Administration or a Master of Arts in Leadership, you might want to progress your career in a leadership role. These classes will all assist you in acquiring the leadership skills listed below.

We are at the forefront of leadership education as the finest, quickest, and most economical online institution in Kansas City, Milwaukee, Phoenix, and neighboring locations. Get in touch with an enrollment adviser right away to learn which program would best suit your requirements.

www.ingramcontent.com/pod-product-compliance
Lightning Source LLC
Chambersburg PA
CBHW071929120726
48001CB00005B/1928